Greetings from New York

Greetings from New York

A Visit to Manhattan in Postcards

Kerry Tucker

Delilah Books ★ New York / Distributed by G. P. Putnam's Sons

ISBN: 0-933328-04-4
Library of Congress Catalog Card Number: 81-67644

Delilah Books
    A Division of Delilah Communications Ltd.
    118 East 25th Street
    New York, N.Y. 10010

Design by Hal Morgan, Inc., Cambridge, Massachusetts
Skyline ornament by Dorothy Yule

Manufactured in the United States of America

Contents

Introduction

YOU ARE ENTERING New York City—home of Vanderbilts, Whitneys, Astors, Diamond Jim Brady, Henry James, Dorothy Parker, the Rockettes, Jackie Onassis, and Liberty Enlightening the World. Teddy Roosevelt was born here, in a brownstone on East 20th Street; the young Jennie Churchill took her daily stroll in Madison Square Park; and Jack Kerouac hammered out *On the Road* in his Chelsea apartment.

The air is thick with ghosts of demolished buildings, previous occupants, and unforgettable incidents. Here is the park where Lillian Russell used to ride her diamond-studded bicycle; Stanford White was shot in the old Madison Square Garden which stood on the next corner; and the first and much revered Pennsylvania Station lived its too short fifty years just a half mile to the north, practically in the shadow of the original Waldorf-Astoria.

The soil here has produced the world's most lavish crop of skyscrapers. No other city can touch the Empire State Building for craftsmanship, the Chrysler Building for Art Deco detail, or the World Trade Center for sheer engineering virtuosity. New York has more than its share of fabulous earthbound buildings, too—Grand Central Terminal dominates forty-eight acres of midtown, the Metropolitan Museum of Art reigns over upper Fifth Avenue like the family matriarch, and the Stock Exchange offers more excitement per square inch than any other building in the world.

It's little wonder, then, that Manhattan attracts so many visitors. Where else can anyone eat in an automat, shop in the world's largest department store, glimpse a movie star on the sidewalk, ice skate, pass a half dozen world-famous buildings, and watch a musical extravaganza all in one after-

noon and within a one-mile radius? Where else can anyone see three cultures in as many minutes simply by taking a taxi through Soho, Little Italy, and Chinatown?

And in what better way than through postcards can the wonders of New York City be shared with friends from out of town or squirreled away for future reference?

New York City, to its very good fortune, has been endlessly and rapturously documented in this miniature art form. The heyday of the American postcard—from about 1900 to 1918—coincided exactly with Manhattan's first tall-building boom, so the city's earliest skyscrapers enjoy immortality in hundreds of variations. Later, the dramatically geometric and streamlined buildings raised during the thirties and forties were just as appropriately

conveyed by that period's vividly colored, sleekly airbrushed linen cards. And the slickly laminated four-color cards that have dominated the market since the fifties are the ideal pictorial vehicle for the austere glass and steel structures of the last quarter-century.

These small pictures vibrate with a sense of time and place. They record the tides of architectural taste, the whole history of streetlamps, the advancement of mass transportation, and the rise of the neon sign. They let us see landmarks that have vanished, parks that have changed, and structures that existed only in their architects' imaginations.

Many of these cards are also marvels of commercial art. The Detroit Company's postcards are examples of some of the finest color printing ever

produced in the United States; the Rotograph Company's misty-looking pictures are strikingly lovely purely in their composition and exquisite use of a pastel palette; and the intensely colored linen cards produced by the Herbco Company, the Acacia Card Company, and others have a disquieting, liquid beauty that approaches the surreal.

Please notice the details that make these postcards acts of creativity as well as historical documents. Postcard artists have always felt compelled to romanticize their subjects; these cards are embellished with tiny American flags, airplanes, beacons, and cloud formations that probably never really existed at all.

The postcards on the following pages will guide you through several

New York Cities—the immigrant's New York, the entrepreneur's New York, the native's New York, the traveler's New York, and, most of all, the romantic's New York. Maybe they will awaken memories or inspire new visits.

Welcome to New York.

Downtown

THE STATUE OF LIBERTY

Liberty Island, Upper New York Bay
Frédéric Auguste Bartholdi, sculptor; Gustave Eiffel, engineer;
Richard Morris Hunt, architect of the pedestal. 1886

This awesome gift from the people of France stands 151 feet from her
sandals to the tip of her torch. Her pedestal, built with $100,000
contributed by the American people, brings her total height to 306
feet.

The statue was first erected in Bartholdi's studio in Paris and officially presented to the American people on July 4, 1874. She was then
knocked down and packed in 210 crates, where she waited for nine
years while her new countrymen raised the funds to reassemble her
on what was then called Bedloe's Island. On the day of the unveiling,
October 28, 1886, the speechmakers' opening remarks were lost in the
cheers and toots that rose from the harbor when the French and
American flags that draped Liberty's face and shoulders were lifted.

Bartholdi modeled Liberty's face on his mother's. For her body,
however, he turned to Jeanne-Emilie Baheux de Puysieux, a dress-
maker's assistant whom he later married.

The statue's statistics are extraordinary. While her copper skin is
only 3/32-inch thick, together with her steel skeleton it brings Liberty's weight to 225 tons. Her right arm is forty-two feet long, her
index fingers are each eight feet long, and her fingernails average
thirteen by ten inches. Each eye measures two and one-half feet
across, her mouth is three feet wide, and her waist is an ample thirty-
five feet thick.

Visitors may take in a dazzling view of New York Harbor from the
windows in Liberty's crown, but her torch has been closed to the
public since 1916 because of traffic jams within her arm.

The information inscribed on the tablet that Liberty holds in her
left hand is surprisingly spare. It just says July IV MDCCLXXVI.

STATUE OF LIBERTY AS ILLUMINATED AT NIGHT, NEW YORK CITY

FORTWOOD.

6A-H2562

UNITED STATES IMMIGRATION STATION/ELLIS ISLAND NATIONAL MONUMENT

Ellis Island, Upper New York Bay
Boring & Tilton, architects. 1900

In 1882 the federal government moved New York's immigration station from Castle Clinton, on the Battery, to a new building on six-acre Ellis Island. That building burned in 1897 and was replaced by Boring and Tilton's whimsically turreted brick and iron facility, where steerage-class immigrants were processed at a rate of nearly ten thousand a day. In 1907, the peak year of immigration, more than 1.2 million new arrivals passed through the station.

A structure known as the "Bath and Laundry Building" could accommodate more than two thousand bathers a day, and each of them was provided with his own towel and a cake of soap while his clothes were being laundered. It was estimated that twenty thousand garments could be disinfected and cleaned daily. The government bill of fare, free to all immigrants, was described by a waiter as "stewed prunes, the stew of all nations, a loaf of bread, and choice of water or diluted coffee."

In 1954 the station was closed after some 14 million immigrants had been processed there. It is now Ellis Island National Monument and may be visited via the Liberty Island Ferry.

U. S. IMMIGRATION STATION, ELLIS ISLAND, NEW YORK.

ADMINISTRATION BUILDING.

New York Harbor, New York

NEW YORK AQUARIUM/CASTLE CLINTON NATIONAL MONUMENT

Battery Park
John McComb, Jr., architect. 1811

John McComb's kidney-shaped fort, the West Battery, was originally situated offshore at the end of a two-hundred-foot causeway (which collapsed during a welcoming ceremony for President Andrew Jackson), but the intervening water has since been filled in. The twenty-eight cannons mounted on the castle were never used, but their mere presence may have had a deterring effect during the War of 1812.

In 1823 the federal government ceded the West Battery to New York City. It was promptly filled with plants and six thousand seats and renamed "Castle Garden," a "place of resort." Here the Marquis de Lafayette was received, memorial services for Napoleon were held, and Jenny Lind, "the Swedish Nightingale," was first heard by an American audience.

From 1855 to 1892 the building served as New York's immigration center, and in 1896, after a remodeling by

15 MAIN FLOOR VIEW, NEW YORK AQUARIUM   COPR. N.Y. ZOOLOGICAL SOCIETY

McKim, Mead and White, it became the New York Aquarium. The aquarium was moved to Coney Island in the early 1940s, the building was designated a national monument by Congress in 1946, and finally, in 1976, it was returned to its original condition and opened to the public.

On December 11, 1896, the aquarium's opening day, more than thirty thousand visitors filed by 78 species of fish, 125 animal forms, and 12 species of aquatic plants. The seals in the central tank were by far the most popular attraction, and, according to one viewer, a police-man kept everyone moving "at a rate that did not allow them to read the labels."

By modern standards the quality of the care given the sea creatures was poor. The aquarium's water supply, direct from the harbor and filtered in what had been the fort's ammunition vault, was polluted by waste from upstream towns and cities. Most of the tropical fish died with the onset of winter, and many were blinded by the glare of the sun through the skylights in their white-tiled tanks.

Trinity Church, N. Y. City.

TRINITY CHURCH
Broadway at Wall Street
Richard Upjohn, architect. 1846

The present Trinity Church was built on the site of two earlier Trinity Churches. The first, erected in 1698, burned in 1776; the second, constructed in 1790, was demolished in 1839. Richard Upjohn's Trinity, embellished with a 284-foot steeple, prevailed as the tallest structure in New York for much of the nineteenth century.

Trinity's churchyard covers two and a half acres and contains the remains of Alexander Hamilton, Robert Fulton, Captain James Lawrence, and William Bradford. Charlotte Temple, a soiled dove whose story was the subject of a two-volume novel, *The History of Charlotte Temple, Founded on Fact* (1801), also rests there.

WALL STREET, NEW YORK

WALL STREET

The center of financial trading in the United States, Wall Street runs along what was the northern edge of the city in its days as a Dutch settlement. In 1653 Peter Stuyvesant, then governor, ordered a wall built there to protect the city from an anticipated attack by the British. The attack finally came in 1664, but from the sea, and the Dutch surrendered without making military use of their wall. New York quickly grew beyond the boundary the Dutch had made, but, even though the wall itself disappeared, its memory lives on as the name of one of the country's most famous streets. A stock exchange office opened at 22 Wall Street in 1792; the one at the present site moved in in 1798, and by the second half of the nineteenth century the street had assumed a commanding position in the nation's economy.

The first great ticker-tape parade started spontaneously on Wall Street when the Armistice was announced on November 11, 1918, and 155 tons of ticker tape, shredded telephone books, and streamers were showered from the windows of the offices above.

Bowling Green, New York.

BOWLING GREEN
At the foot of Broadway

The grandfather of all New York City parks, Bowling Green was used as a parade ground and cattle market by the Dutch in the latter half of the seventeenth century. In 1732 the city Common Council leased it at the rate of one peppercorn a year to John Chambers, Peter Bayard, and Peter Jay for use as a bowling green, and Manhattan's first public park was born.

On July 9, 1776, New Yorkers pulled down the park's gilded lead statue of George III and used it for bullets; a fountain now stands in its place. The iron fence that once enclosed the statue met a happier end; only the royal crowns that topped the pickets were destroyed.

VIEW OF LOWER NEW YORK
FROM AIRSHIP
KEY ON OTHER SIDE

HIGH FLYERS FROM COAST TO COAST USE

LASH'S BITTERS

THE GREAT
TONIC LAXATIVE

COPYRIGHT 1911
C. BOHAM
NEW YORK

LOWER MANHATTAN FROM THE AIR

In 1909 Wilbur Wright made the first airplane flight that could be seen from Manhattan; he soared from Governor's Island to Grant's Tomb as part of the Hudson-Fulton Celebration. But the first flight directly over Manhattan was not made until 1911, when Cal Rogers, financed by the Armour Company, flew over the city with advertisements for Vin Fiz, Armour's new grape soft drink, stenciled on the wings and tail of his plane.

By 1911 Manhattan had become famous for its cluster of skyscrapers, and a newspaper account of Rogers's feat praised his courage ". . . in flying directly over the city with its death trap of tall buildings, spires, ragged roofs, and narrow streets."

After a night in nearby Middletown, Rogers continued his flight west and became the first flyer to cross the country. He suffered twelve serious crashes along the way, and, when he finally landed in California, he hobbled triumphantly into the Pacific on crutches.

NEW YORK CITY SKYSCRAPERS

The word "skyscraper" was first used to describe the tallest mast on a clipper ship, but by the turn of the century the term had come to mean the ten-and-more-story buildings shooting heavenward all over New York City.

With the advent of the elevator, New York structures began to attain previously undreamed-of heights. The Tower and Tribune buildings led the trend; the Park Row Building, the Flatiron, the Metropolitan Life Tower, the Singer Building, and the Woolworth Building chased close on their heels. Soon downtown Manhattan looked like a city of needles, and futurists predicted a neck-craner's heaven—a city crammed with towers and tiered sidewalks, all linked by an elaborate network of elevated railways, pedestrian bridges, and commuter airplanes.

PARK ROW BUILDING

15 Park Row
R. H. Robertson, architect. 1899

A very early entry in New York's skyscraper race, the twin-turreted Park Row Building was completed at 390 feet in 1899 (the same year the Eiffel Tower went up) and remained the city's tallest structure until it surrendered the title to the Singer Building at the completion of its steel frame in 1907. The Park Row's construction, a considerable undertaking for its time, involved driving four thousand piles through forty feet of sand to hit bedrock.

Four enormous caryatids (not yet in place in this view) stand watch from the building's fourth floor.

PARK ROW BUILDING, NEW YORK

25

SINGER BUILDING, BY NIGHT, NEW YORK CITY.

THE SINGER TOWER

149 Broadway at Liberty Street
Ernest Flagg, architect. 1908. Demolished
1970

This eclectic assemblage of terra cotta and steel was an addition to the original Singer Building at Liberty and Broadway. Ernest Flagg, who was also responsible for the Charles Scribner's Sons bookstore on Fifth Avenue, raised the original structure five stories and added a building with a frontage of seventy-six feet on Broadway. For a time the 612-foot Singer Building was the tallest in the world, and its elevators could make the trip from the ground to the forty-second-story observation area in one minute flat. It was demolished to make way for One Liberty Plaza, a 772-foot shaft of steel and glass.

THE WOOLWORTH BUILDING
233 Broadway between Barclay Street and
Park Place
Cass Gilbert, architect. 1913

F. W. Woolworth spent $13.5 million in
nickels and dimes on this "cathedral of com-
merce" modeled on London's House of Par-
liament, which he greatly admired. At 791½
feet the Woolworth Building was the world's
tallest for almost twenty years.

Woolworth spared no expense. He lined
the foyer with marble imported from the Isle
of Skyros, made certain that each of the
building's twenty-eight elevators had a telephone, and oversaw the installation of a
basement swimming pool. For the building's opening ceremonies President Wood-
row Wilson illuminated its fifty-five stories
with eighty thousand electric lights by
pressing a button in the White House.

In 1941 the United States Navy ordered
the observation tower closed because it offered too good a view of the ships in the
harbor. It has never been reopened.

Woolworth Building,
New York.
Highest Office Building
in the World.
55 Stories.
750 feet high.

Copyright Littig & Co., N. Y.

Irving Trust Co. Building, New York.

THE IRVING TRUST COMPANY BUILDING

1 Wall Street between Broadway and New Street
Voorhees, Gmelin & Walker, architects.
1931

On the morning of March 22, 1931, the Irving Trust Company moved $3 billion in gold, securities, and currency eight blocks through the winding streets of lower Manhattan to its new building, and every pedestrian and automobile passing through the area was in direct machine-gun range for the two hours it took to make the transfer. But nothing untoward happened, and the treasure was deposited intact in what was then the third largest vault in the world, exceeded in size only by those of the Bank of England and the New York Federal Reserve Bank. The vault, sunk seventy-two feet into bedrock, was lined with six feet of concrete, iron, steel, and a sheet of solidified chemicals which, according to the bank, would give off paralyzing fumes under the heat of a cracksman's torch.

The bank was named for Washington Irving and occupies the site on which the writer shared an office with his brother and wrote *Diedrich Knickerbocker's History of New York.*

THE WORLD TRADE CENTER

Bounded by Church, Liberty, West, and
Vesey streets
Minoru Yamasaki & Associates; Emery
Roth & Sons, architects. 1973

The tallest buildings in New York and the
second tallest in the world, the 1,350-foot
twin towers of the World Trade Center were
built by the Port Authority of New York and
New Jersey to bring together businesses involved in international trade. The buildings
contain 10 million square feet of office
space—seven times the area in the Empire
State Building—and two hundred thousand
tons of concrete—enough to build a five-
foot-wide sidewalk from Wall Street to
Washington, D. C. Fifty thousand people—
more than twice the population of Monaco—
work inside.

The twin towers pose an irresistible chal-
lenge to adventurers, chief among them
mountain climber George Willig, the "hu-
man fly," who scaled the South Tower on
May 26, 1977.

THE BROOKLYN BRIDGE

The East River, from City Hall Park in Manhattan to
Cadman Plaza in Brooklyn
John A. and Colonel Washington Roebling, engineers.
1883

No single structure more dramatically illustrates the triumph of technology in the nineteenth century than the Brooklyn Bridge. Massive in its conception and modern in its engineering, the bridge has always thrilled the public imagination. It was the longest of the few successful suspension bridges of its time and remained so for twenty years. It was the first bridge to span the East River, the first to use steel cables, and one of the first to use pneumatic caissons for underwater construction. For a time its towers were taller than every other building in New York except the steeple of Trinity Church.

The strength of the bridge rests on the revolutionary use of steel cables manufactured at the construction site in continuous, 185-mile lengths. The technique was invented by John Roebling, the engineer of the bridge and a cable manufacturer. In all, 6.8 million pounds of steel cable were used.

John Roebling died in 1869, six months after construction began, of gangrene resulting from a ferry accident on a Brooklyn pier, and Colonel Washington Roebling, his son, took his place. Soon he too succumbed to an accident in his work on the bridge. An expert in caisson disease, or "the bends," Washington Roebling contracted the disease himself in 1872 and was confined to bed for the final years of construction. His wife, Emily, acted as his messenger, and some think that she was in effect the chief engineer during the final phase of the work.

G 8b. Brooklyn Bridge.

Transportation Center, New York City.

THE BROOKLYN BRIDGE TERMINAL

The east side of City Hall Park at the Manhattan terminus of the Brooklyn Bridge
Hoppin, Koen & Huntington, architects. Planned in 1911. Never completed

As trolley traffic back and forth over the Brooklyn Bridge became heavier in the early days of the century, it created a congestion problem at the trolley station at the end of the bridge, where passengers changed to the Interborough and other train lines. An enormous transportation terminal was designed, and $500,000 was appropriated for work to begin in 1911. But the new Manhattan and Williamsburg bridges and the soon-to-be-completed subway tunnels to Brooklyn were already taking much of the pressure off what had been the city's only link to Brooklyn; the subway station was the only part of the bridge terminal plan to actually materialize.

E-1202. City Hall, New York, N. Y.

CITY HALL

City Hall Park, between Broadway and Park Row
Mangin & McComb, architects. 1811

Mangin and McComb won a $350 prize when they submitted their plans for this building to the 1802 City Hall design competition. Mangin designed the facade and McComb the interior, but Mayor DeWitt Clinton gets the credit for the myopic decision to face the north side with Newark brownstone rather than the Massachusetts marble that graced the other sides of the structure. He had to cut costs somewhere, and, after all, no one of consequence lived north of Chambers Street. Both the marble and the sandstone were stripped away and replaced by Alabama limestone and Minnesota granite in 1954, ensuring an equal view to all.

2041 — Mulberry St., New York.

MULBERRY STREET

Running from Canal to Spring streets, Mulberry is the backbone of Manhattan's Little Italy. The tenements along this street have housed the Italian-American community for nearly a century.

The great wave of Italian immigration to the United States took place between 1880 and 1910, when poverty, overpopulation, and epidemics of cholera and malaria forced more than 3 million Italians from their homeland. New York, as the main port of entry, also became a stopping place, and Mulberry Street, stretching down through what is now Chinatown, became a home for many of the new Americans. Many of their descendants have moved out of Manhattan, leaving the area to newer arrivals from China and Puerto Rico.

Today the Mulberry Street area is noted for its excellent restaurants, sidewalk cafés, and the spectacular Feast of San Gennaro, which takes place very year in mid-September.

THE WILLIAMSBURG BRIDGE

The East River, from Delancey and Clinton streets in
Manhattan to Washington Plaza in Brooklyn
Leffert L. Buck, engineer. 1903

In its day the Williamsburg Bridge was the longest suspension bridge in the world. Its 135-foot clearance was
two feet higher than the Brooklyn Bridge's, and its six-
teen-hundred-foot span five feet longer.

Ten seconds after the bridge opened at 5:00 A.M. on
December 21, 1903, "Wally" Owen sped past the toll
collector toward Manhattan in his fifty-six-horsepower
automobile. Once over the bridge he spun around and
returned to Brooklyn to become the first person to cross
in each direction. He carried as a passenger a reporter
from the New York Times, who clocked the round trip
at six minutes, fifty seconds. Several policemen wandering about on the dark roadway barely escaped injury.
Less dangerous were the pedestrians who ran a wild
footrace to become the first person across. Other firsts
during the morning included a bicyclist who made the
trip riding backward and a man who hopped across on
one foot.

2048 — Hester Street, New York.

HESTER STREET

The Lower East Side at the turn of the century was a bustling neighborhood of Jewish immigrants, most of whom had been driven from Central and Eastern Europe by war and persecution. By 1910 about a million Jews lived in New York, more than half of them in a twenty-block area around Hester Street. Crowded into stifling tenements over streets packed with pushcarts, many of these immigrants worked in the neighborhood's garment industry. Though marked by poverty, the Lower East Side was also alive with intellectual and cultural activity. Cafés and lecture halls were the scenes of discussions on the issues of the day, and year after year the branch library in the neighborhood reported the highest rate of book circulation in the city.

Every Sunday Hester Street still bustles with the activity of street venders, and it is still peopled with recent Jewish immigrants—from the Soviet Union, Cuba, Egypt, Iran, Israel, and other countries.

Manhattan Bridge Approach, New York City.

MANHATTAN BRIDGE
The East River, from Canal Street and the Bowery in
Manhattan to Flatbush Avenue Extension in Brooklyn
Gustave Lindenthal, engineer. 1909
Approach Plaza, Manhattan side
Carrère & Hastings, architects. 1912

Bitter complaints were heard when the name "Manhattan Bridge" was announced. The *New York Times*
called it "meaningless and indistinct," and pointed out

that "all bridges across the East River are Manhattan
bridges." Nevertheless, the name stuck.

Fierce political disputes raged over the engineer's
design. A new commissioner took charge in the middle
of the project and tried to replace the original plan with
his own, highly suspect, design. He didn't succeed. His
successor was more concerned with the approach to the
bridge and managed to design and construct the plaza
without political interference. The square trees pictured
here were never grown in the park.

37

Pell Street, New York

CHINATOWN

Bounded by East Broadway and Canal and Baxter streets

The first Chinese came to New York in the 1840s and 50s; they were sailors who jumped ship, fortune seekers who had come to California during the gold rush, and workers imported to help build the transcontinental railroad. Chinatown in its early days was clustered around the corner of Mott and Pell streets, and its population was made up largely of men, many of whom worked as cigar makers, launderers, or sandwich-board carriers. As immigration increased, Chinese shops, restaurants, and newspapers sprang up, as did a mysterious underworld of opium dens, gambling parlors, and trade in white slaves. The Tong wars in the early days of the century taxed the abilities of New York's most assiduous police detectives.

Chinatown remains a bustling, colorful neighborhood teeming with sidewalk vendors, small shops, and a dazzling array of restaurants.

G 132a Cooper Union. N Y City

COOPER UNION

The Bowery at 7th Street
Frederick A. Peterson, architect. 1859

Peter Cooper began his working life at the age of seventeen as an apprentice to a carriage maker who paid him board and twenty-five dollars a year. From that grim start grew his copper, glue, iron, and locomotive empire, estimated in the 1850s at a value of $2 million. Out of gratitude to the city that had made his career possible, Cooper created the Cooper Union, a tuition-free institution open to all who passed the entrance exams. The school's stated purpose was to give its students the skills necessary for earning a living in trade and the useful arts. Cooper Union continues to fulfill that purpose, but primarily as an art school. The building's Great Hall has been the scene of many of New York's most historic events, including the speech that Abraham Lincoln himself credited with gaining him the presidency and those meetings that launched the American Red Cross, the Volunteers of America, and the NAACP.

Washington Arch, New York City.

WASHINGTON MEMORIAL ARCH

Washington Square, at the south end of
Fifth Avenue
McKim, Mead & White, architects. 1892

To celebrate the 1889 centennial of George
Washington's inauguration, Stanford White
designed a wood and plaster arch that
spanned Fifth Avenue at Madison Square.
It was so popular that the public demanded
a permanent arch, and a local fund-raising
committee produced the money to have
White redesign his original work for execu-
tion in marble.

This view is of the south side of the arch.
Statues of Washington in two moods flank
the other side; *Washington in Peace* by A.
Stirling Calder on the west, and *Washington
in War* by Hermon A. MacNeil on the east.

Washington Square North, the street that
faces the north side of the arch, has housed
some of New York's most illustrious citizens,
among them Edith Wharton, Henry James,
John Dos Passos, and Rockwell Kent.

JEFFERSON MARKET

425 Sixth Avenue at West 10th Street
Vaux & Withers, architects. 1877

In 1873 the motley assortment of buildings
that stood on this site—including a wooden
fire tower and a municipal market—was torn
down to make room for a trio of architectur-
ally harmonious buildings—a jail, a courthouse, and another municipal market. The
courthouse is all that remains today.

Voted the fifth most beautiful building in
the country by a national poll of architects
in 1885 (it lagged behind Trinity Church in
Boston, the United States Capitol, W. K.
Vanderbilt's Fifth Avenue mansion, and
New York's Trinity Church), the acutely Vic-
torian courthouse was the scene of many
dark events in New York social history, including Harry Thaw's arraignment for the
murder of Stanford White. Abandoned as a
courthouse in 1945, the structure slowly deteriorated until persistent local residents
persuaded the city to restore it; it now
houses a branch of the New York Public
Library.

41

5677. GRACE CHURCH, NEW YORK.

GRACE CHURCH

800 Broadway at East 10th Street
James Renwick, Jr., architect. 1846

James Renwick, Jr., who later designed St. Patrick's Cathedral, was only twenty-five when he drew up the plans for Grace Church, an elegant white marble structure that for years figured prominently in northward views of the city.

The church was also the favored site for fashionable society weddings. When General Tom Thumb and Lavinia Warren—P. T. Barnum's tiny "Queen of Beauty"—were married here on February 10, 1863, Broadway from 10th Street to Union Square was crowded the entire day with onlookers hoping for a peek at the diminutive pair. The bride wore a white satin gown trimmed with lace half a yard wide, a veil trimmed to match, and white satin slippers adorned with seed pearls and satin rosettes. She was attended by her sister, Minnie Warren, sixteen years old and at the time the smallest woman in the world. The reception was held at the Metropolitan Hotel, and the couple honeymooned in England.

Midtown

Union Square, New York.

UNION SQUARE
Bounded by East 14th and East 17th streets, Union Square West, and Park Avenue South

As businesses took over the established residential neighborhoods in the southernmost part of Manhattan, the wealthy rebuilt their homes at what was then the northern edge of the city. By the 1840s Union Square had become one of the most fashionable residential areas in New York, and many of its mansions boasted silver door handles, extravagant plate-glass windows, and elaborate indoor plumbing.

But the city continued to grow, and the wealthy were forced to flee to the north once again. First hotels, then boardinghouses, and finally shops invaded the Union Square area, and by the 1870s it was a glittering shopping district. Richard Harding Davis described the square in 1892: "private carriages line the curb in quadruple lines, and the pavement is impressively studded with white-breeched grooms." The area also teemed with other attractions; an 1870 guidebook counted fifteen "temples of love" at the square's southern end.

The Siegel-Cooper Department Store, New York.

SIEGEL COOPER BUILDING

616–632 Sixth Avenue between West 18th and West 19th streets
DeLemos & Cordes, architects. 1896

When Siegel Cooper & Co. of Chicago decided to build the most lavish department store in New York, it chose a site on Sixth Avenue just above 14th Street. B. Altman's stood across the way, Macy's was four blocks south, and Stern's and O'Neill's were located just to the north. Soon the new store outshone them all.

On opening night 150,000 people gathered outside to see the electric lights that spelled out "The Big Store." Inside seven floors containing fifteen and a half acres of space overflowed with merchandise ranging from exotic foods to clothes and hardware, or, as the store boasted—"everything from needles to elephants." And there really was an elephant. It was sold to a zoological park on East 14th Street two weeks after the store opened.

The store eventually fell on hard times. It was converted into a hospital during World War I and has been used for warehousing and light industry ever since.

12740 METROPOLITAN BUILDING, NEW YORK.　　HEIGHT 700 FEET

THE METROPOLITAN LIFE TOWER

1 Madison Avenue between East 23rd and
East 24th streets
Napoleon LeBrun & Sons, architects. 1909

The Metropolitan Life Insurance Company
was one of the first large businesses to use
its headquarters as a corporate symbol. In-
spired by the Campanile of Venice (pictured
on the "Wonders of the World" card at the
right), the Metropolitan Life Building's
tower is 75 feet wide on Madison Avenue,
85 feet wide on 24th Street, and 657 feet tall,
and for several years it reigned as the tallest
office building in the world.

The tower's promoters boasted that its
four-faced clock was the largest in the world,
larger even than Big Ben. To this day its
bells sound a measure by Handel on the
quarter hour. The light at the top of the
tower still flashes one, two, three, or four
times in red to indicate the quarter hour and
in white after the fourth red flash to tell the
hour.

THE WONDERS OF THE WORLD.

The Metropolitan Life Tower played a key role in New York's skyscraper race, a race at one time dominated by the 284-foot spire of Trinity Church. The eleven-story Tribune Building in 1873 and the steel-framed Tower Building in 1889 had challenged Trinity's needle, but the church spire claimed supremacy until 1890, when the New York *World* built a 309-foot office building opposite City Hall. In 1899 the Park Row Building took the lead at 390 feet and became the tallest building in New York and the third tallest in the world—outdone only by Cologne Cathedral and the Eiffel Tower. The Singer Building reached 612 feet in 1907, only to be bested after two years by the Metropolitan Life Tower. The Woolworth Building put a decisive end to the race for many years when it was topped off in 1913 at 791½ feet.

47

MADISON SQUARE

Bounded by Fifth and Madison avenues and East 23rd and East 26th streets

In the mid-nineteenth century Madison Square was the most fashionable address in Manhattan. Then hotels and restaurants crowded out homes, and the square became a popular place for dining and entertainment. Delmonico's, considered by many the finest restaurant in the city, moved to Madison Square in 1876 and remained there for twenty years, catering to the wealthiest palates in the country. Some of the city's most luxurious hotels grew up around the square, including the Hoffman House, the Brunswick, and the Fifth Avenue Hotel. New York's first men's club, the Union Club, was situated just to the south at 21st Street.

With the building of Madison Square Garden and the Metropolitan Life Tower, Madison Square entered a different phase in its life—that of a tourist attraction.

Four statues stand in the park. The one of William Seward, Secretary of War under Lincoln, was sculpted by Randolph Rogers. Only the head is actually Seward's; as an economy measure, the sculptor substituted the body from a figure of Lincoln that he had on hand. In fact, if you look carefully at the statue you will notice that Seward holds the Emancipation Proclamation in his left hand.

Rainy Day at Madison Square, New York City

MADISON SQUARE GARDEN
Madison Square to Park Avenue between East 26th and East 27th streets
McKim, Mead & White, architects. 1890. Demolished 1925

In its time Madison Square Garden was the largest amphitheater in the world, and many of New York's most spectacular and extraordinary events occurred there. They include a reenactment of the Battle of Santiago complete with ocean; one-legged bicyclist Charles Kilpatrick's daredevil leap over a twenty-foot crevice; and the mercy killing of what was then the world's largest elephant. "Dick," a member of the Forepaugh and Sells Circus, developed "elephant madness" and was strangled in the basement of the garden at the hands of forty men.

The most sensational event linked with the Garden was the murder of its architect, Stanford White, in 1906. The mad Harry Thaw, husband of White's former mistress Evelyn Nesbitt, shot White in the head as he watched a performance of "Mam'zelle Champagne" in the roof garden. Thaw was later acquitted of the murder and confined to an insane asylum.

The eighteen-foot copper statue of Diana by Augustus Saint-Gaudens, which originally topped the tower, was removed in 1893 at the insistence of White and the sculptor, who thought she was too fat for the slender tower. The original figure was replaced with a more sylphlike thirteen-foot version. Her cape, a big sheet of copper, swung her around in the wind, and she was known irreverently as the world's largest weathervane.

When the imminent destruction of the Garden was announced in 1924, an anguished public looked frantically for a new home for Diana. For a time it seemed she would go to the New York City Museum; or to the New York Life Insurance Building; or to New York University. Finally she found refuge at the Philadelphia Museum of Art and is still there today.

Madison Square Garden, New York.

51

HOTEL CHELSEA
WEST TWENTY-THIRD STREET AT SEVENTH AVENUE
NEW YORK
Fireproof. Rate of fire insurance one-fifth of one per cent.
Room with bath adjoining, $1.00 and $1.50   Room with private bath, $2.00
Suites—$3.00 to $10.00 a day
500 ROOMS   ALL OUTSIDE ROOMS   400 BATHS
Restaurant a la Carte   Table d'Hote   Club breakfasts

THE CHELSEA HOTEL

222 West 23rd Street between Seventh and
Eighth avenues
Hubert, Pirsson & Company, architects.
1884

The Chelsea Hotel was originally the Chelsea Apartments, one of the city's largest and most luxurious apartment buildings and the first to offer residences on a cooperative basis. It was billed as the most fireproof apartment house in the city; Philip Hubert had covered all the wood supporting beams with fireproof blocks or cement, ensuring that any fire would be contained within one apartment.

In 1905 the Chelsea Apartments became the Chelsea Hotel and a favorite stopping place for artists, writers, and actors, among them Edgar Lee Masters, Dylan Thomas, Sarah Bernhardt, Thomas Wolfe, Tennessee Williams, Jane Fonda, and Yevgeny Yevtushenko. It was also the scene of Andy Warhol's 1966 movie *Chelsea Girls*.

THE FLATIRON BUILDING

23rd Street at the intersection of Broadway
and Fifth Avenue
D. H. Burnham & Co., architects. 1902

The peculiarly shaped Flatiron Building,
which looms over the intersection of Broadway and Fifth Avenue like a monstrous
tombstone, was one of the first buildings in
New York constructed with a supporting
steel frame. The apex of its triangle is also
one of the windiest spots in the city, and it
is said that the term "Twenty-three skidoo"
was coined by policemen in their efforts to
rid the corner of men who habitually looked
up ladies' skirts lifted by the wind.

For years the Flatiron served as the flag-
ship of New York's skyscraper fleet, both
because of its dramatic contours and because
of the technical advances it represented. It
has also proved irresistible to photogra-
phers; both Edward Steichen and Alfred
Stieglitz made it the subject of memorable
photographs.

FLAT IRON BUILDING, NEW-YORK.

53

K 1209

THE LITTLE CHURCH AROUND THE CORNER/EPISCOPAL CHURCH OF THE TRANSFIGURATION

1 East 29th Street between Fifth and Madison avenues
Architect unknown, 1849–1861; Frederick Clarke Withers, architect of the Lady and Mortuary chapels, 1908

This demure little church, built from the plans of an unknown architect, is the only example in New York of the fourteenth-century Cottage Gothic style. It is also the only New York church with a lich gate—a covered resting place at the entrance to the churchyard.

When actor George Holland died in 1870, his friend Joseph Jefferson asked the minister at a fashionable church to perform the funeral service. The minister turned up his nose and directed Jefferson to "the little church around the corner." The name stuck and the church has remained a favored place of worship for theater people. Edwin Booth, Otis Skinner, Dame Ellen Terry, Sarah Bernhardt, and Sir Henry Irving all were affiliated with the church at one time or another.

THE WALDORF-ASTORIA HOTEL

Northwest corner of Fifth Avenue and 33rd Street

Henry J. Hardenbergh, architect. 1893 and 1897. Demolished for the Empire State Building 1929

From 1857 to 1893 the block where the Empire State Building now stands was the site of two mansions belonging to the Astor family; one was owned by New York's social dictator Caroline Schermerhorn Astor, and the other belonged to her nephew, William Waldorf Astor, who loathed his aunt. To spite her, when he and his wife moved to Germany, they left instructions that their house be razed and that the thirteen-story Hotel Waldorf be built in its place. The outraged Caroline Astor threatened to build the world's largest stable next door for revenge, but had second thoughts and erected instead the adjoining Astoria. The twin hotels flourished from 1893 until 1929 as the most fashionable stopping place in Manhattan.

The hotel offered a replica of an Astor dining room, luxurious period rooms, and a carrier pigeon service between its roof and the Bellevue-Stratford in Philadelphia. It took the pigeons three hours to make the round trip.

John Jacob Raskob and his partners spent nearly five months and $900,000 to demolish the Waldorf-Astoria. Its remnants were dumped in the Atlantic fifteen miles beyond Sandy Hook.

Hotel Waldorf Astoria, New York

Pennsylvania Railroad Station, 7th Ave. and 33d St., New York.

PENNSYLVANIA STATION

Seventh to Eighth avenues between 31st and 33rd streets
McKim, Mead & White, architects. 1910. Demolished 1963

Pennsylvania Station was probably McKim, Mead and White's greatest achievement. Built at a cost of $90 million and fashioned after the ancient Baths of Cara-calla in Rome, it covered nearly eight acres and contained what was at the time the world's largest waiting room, which measured 320 by 110 feet; the vaulted ceiling was 150 feet high. Two smaller waiting rooms, one for men and the other for women, adjoined it on the west side.

Many consider Pennsylvania Station the most magnificent building ever erected in New York City; certainly the elegant steel and glass domes and the arches

13640. CONCOURSE, PENNSYLVANIA STATION, NEW YORK.   COPR. DETROIT PUBLISHING CO.

of its train concourse formed one of the most fascinating blends of classical design and modern technology in the history of American architecture.

"Until the first blow fell," said the *New York Times* in 1963, "no one was convinced that Pennsylvania Station would be demolished or that New York would permit this monumental act of vandalism against one of the largest and finest landmarks of its age of Roman elegance. Somehow someone would surely find a way to prevent it at the last minute. . . ." But no one did, and the last of the rubble was brushed away in 1966 to make way for what is the most recent Madison Square Garden. A few salvaged pieces—a column base, a capital, and a figure that once supported one side of an enormous clock—now stand in the Frieda Schiff Warburg Sculpture Garden at the Brooklyn Museum.

Hudson and Manhattan Tube,
New York City.

by Brown Bros., N. Y.

THE HUDSON RIVER TUNNELS

Pennsylvania Station was the crowning glory of a new tunnel system—a visible monument to unseen wonders. Starting in 1910, trains passed from the station, through the North River Tunnel, and under the Hudson to points south and west. Through the East River Tunnel trains passed to Long Island and New England, and passengers riding from Boston to Philadelphia could travel smoothly under the center of Manhattan, unseen and undisturbed by the bustle of activity above.

The McAdoo Tunnel, built in 1907 and now used by the PATH trains to New Jersey, was the first to cross under the Hudson River. To celebrate the completion of the work, the tunnel's sponsors hosted a dinner at Sherry's for all employees. Five hundred attended, including engineers, rodmen, walking bosses, draftsmen, drillers, and sand hogs. After the speeches had been made and cigars passed around, the Sand Hog Band took the stage, dressed in yellow oilskin suits, long rubber boots, and yellow tunneling hats.

The Pennsylvania Railroad opened its tunnel with a decidedly less populist spirit. A month before the tube was officially inaugurated a private car carrying J. P. Morgan and a few of his guests traveled the length of the completed tunnel.

Today New York City has 134 miles of subway tunnels, a mere drop in the underground bucket compared to the city's 7,800 miles of gas mains and 20 million miles of buried wire for telephones.

MACY'S DEPARTMENT STORE

West 34th to West 35th streets between
Broadway and Seventh Avenue
DeLemos & Cordes, architects of the
original Broadway building, 1902; Robert
D. Kohn, architect of the new Seventh
Avenue building, 1931

When Macy's moved from 14th Street to
34th Street in 1902, the new store's promoters boasted that if the building's entire floor
area were divided into fifty-by-twenty-five-
foot shops strung side by side, they would
make frontage equal to the distance from
18th Street to 125th Street. In 1931 the store
grew even larger—and is now so immense
that it bills itself as "the world's largest
store." If it weren't for the fact that Robert
Smith, a competitor of Macy's, bought the
building on the southeast corner of the lot
in 1900, and that his estate refuses to part
with it, Macy's would cover the entire block
on which it stands. Smith's lot is now occupied by a Nedick's hot-dog stand.

Macy's is famous for its spectacular annual
Thanksgiving Day parades; they began in
1924 and have always featured enormous
helium balloons. In 1932 a certain Annette
Gibson snagged a sixty-foot yellow tomcat
with the wing of her biplane during a flying
lesson, while thousands watched in horror
from below. With the plane eighty feet
above the ground, the flying instructor took
over the controls and managed to nose the
craft up again. The *New York Times* reported
Miss Gibson "quite unshaken by the inci-
dent."

R. H. Macy Company, New York, N. Y.

Midtown and Empire State Building
New York

THE EMPIRE STATE BUILDING

350 Fifth Avenue at 34th Street
Shreve, Lamb & Harmon, architects. 1931

The Empire State Building may no longer be New York City's tallest building, but it is still the undisputed queen of the Manhattan skyline. It still holds the record for the world's fastest-rising skyscraper; work began in March 1930 and ended only thirteen months later, thanks to a daily crew of over twenty-five hundred workers. Fourteen of them died during the construction.

The dirigible mooring mast, at first considered one of the building's chief attractions, turned out to be a disappointing gimmick. In 1931 a privately owned dirigi-

ble tied up for three precarious minutes, and two weeks later a Navy blimp dropped some newspapers off, but the tremendous updrafts threatened the safety of all involved and no further mooring attempts were ever made.

From its Fifth Avenue doorstep to the top of its television tower the Empire State Building measures a breathtaking 1,472 feet. The building's other statistics are just as astounding. It contains sixty-five hundred windows; four hundred firehose connections; seven miles of elevator shafts; fifty miles of radiator pipe; two hundred thousand cubic feet of stone; and 2,158,000 square feet of floor space for offices.

The Empire State has braved its share of disasters: in 1945 an Army B-25 bomber crashed into the building's north side at the seventy-ninth floor, killing fourteen and injuring twenty-six. And in 1937 King Kong scaled the skyscraper, terrorizing moviegoers by the millions.

THE CHRYSLER BUILDING
405 Lexington Avenue between 42nd and 43rd streets
William Van Alen, architect. 1930

This stunning tribute to the Art Deco style would have been crowned with a blunt dome had the spirit of competition not spurred Walter Chrysler to greater heights. He had instructed Van Alen to build the tallest building in the world, and the same command had been given to H. Craig Severance by the owners of the Bank of Manhattan, which was rising fast at 40 Wall Street. Van Alen had originally planned to stop the Chrysler at 925 feet, but revised his blueprints when Severance announced that his building would stop at 927 feet. The Wall Street building was finished first, its sponsors confident that they had created the tallest building in the world. Then Van Alen raised the Chrysler's spire, which had been assembled in secret inside an elevator shaft. The building went on record at a total height of 1,048 feet. Its reign as the world's tallest building was brief; less than two years later the Empire State Building sped skyward and took the title.

The Chrysler's interior is as dazzling as its facade. The lobby is almost feverish with Art Deco detail—the ceilings, the floors, the lighting fixtures, the elevator cabs—even the radiators—are unified by sleek, angular patterns inlaid in wood, marble, and stainless steel, all fastidiously crafted.

The Cloud Club, once the most exclusive luncheon club in the Grand Central area, occupied three of the Chrysler Building's upper floors and offered its members a ticker-tape room, an elegant dining room, overnight accommodations, and a men's room with the best view of any such facility in Manhattan. The club was eventually limited to one floor and in 1979 ceased operating altogether.

K4844

Grand Central Terminal Station, New York City.

GRAND CENTRAL TERMINAL

42nd Street at Park Avenue
Reed & Stem and Warren & Wetmore, architects. 1913

Truly grand in its conception, the terminal is more amazing for its hidden wonders than for its obvious splendor. It occupies forty-eight acres of midtown property, almost all of it underground. From east of Madison Avenue to Lexington Avenue, from 42nd to 50th streets, the buildings around the station are basementless and conceal thirty-four miles of railroad track. To the north the tracks run discreetly beneath Park Avenue.

By submerging the tracks and yard the builders reclaimed land worth tens of millions of dollars at the time and an untold fortune today. The work involved in

70982 GRAND CENTRAL TERMINAL, NEW YORK, MAIN CONCOURSE   COPR. DETROIT PUBLISHING CO.

this massive excavation is almost unthinkable. Between 1903 and 1913, four hundred railroad cars loaded with dirt were hauled away from the site each day. When the terminal opened in 1913, it was estimated to have cost almost half as much as the Panama Canal.

The station itself is of fantastic proportions. It was designed to accommodate 100 million passengers a year, but its capacity has never been tested. The great arrival and departure concourse has a vaulted ceiling 125 feet high, on which is painted a map of the constellations. On the heavenly blue background, coated evenly by fifty painters working in one stretch, are painted twenty-five hundred stars of various magnitude, sixty-three illuminated by electricity. There are so many

clocks in the building that it takes seven men working overtime to quickly switch them to or from Daylight Savings Time.

When the station opened, the main waiting room was far more elegantly appointed than it is today, and the traveler could find a host of conveniences nearby—barber shops, manicure parlors, baths, and private rooms complete with valet service for men and maids for women. A barber could be reserved by telegraph and be found awaiting his client's arrival in a private room. John W. Campbell once kept a private apartment in the station for entertaining guests; that space now houses the Grand Central Police headquarters.

United Nations Headquarters and East River, New York City.   UN3

THE UNITED NATIONS HEADQUARTERS

First Avenue between East 42nd and East 48th streets
The United Nations Board of Design, headed by
Wallace K. Harrison, architects. 1952

Before accepting John D. Rockefeller, Jr.'s, donation of
an $8.5 million site on the East River, the United Na-
tions considered building its headquarters in San Francisco, Westchester County, and Connecticut and had
various temporary quarters, including Rockefeller Center, Hunter College, the Sperry Gyroscope Plant, and

the New York City Building left over from the 1939
World's Fair in Queens.

The organization's design team, which included
France's Le Corbusier, Brazil's Oscar Niemeyer, and
Australia's G. A. Souilheux, considered fifty-two designs
before settling on a plan for a sleek, imposing glass and
marble complex dominated by the 550-foot-tall Secretariat Building. The low, gently curved building to the
north of the Secretariat houses the General Assembly;
the smaller rectangular building to the south (not yet
built in this view) is the Dag Hammarskjöld Library.

Reservoir.   NEW YORK.

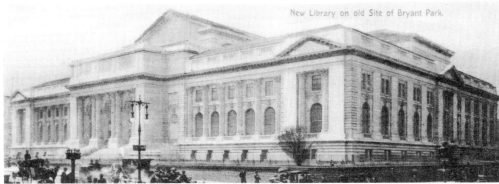

New Library on old Site of Bryant Park.

THE NEW YORK PUBLIC LIBRARY
Fifth Avenue between 40th and 42nd streets
Carrère & Hastings, architects. 1911

In 1900 the Croton Reservoir was demolished to allow the construction of the New York Public Library—a consolidation of the Astor Library, the Lenox Library, and the Tilden Trust. The building, a monumental example of the Beaux-Arts style, opened to the public on May 25, 1911. That day fifty thousand people came to marvel at the library's 295-foot long reading room, its ninety miles of shelf space, and its new, labor-saving system of calling up books, which involved sealing request slips in capsules that were whisked through pneumatic tubes to the stacks—a system still in use.

The two pink Tennessee marble lions that now flank the library steps—known to some passersby as Patience and Fortitude and to others as Lord and Lady Astor—were sculpted by Edward C. Potter. They protect what has become a massive and world-renowned collection of books, newspapers, maps, manuscripts, periodicals, prints, and photographs.

THE AMERICAN RADIATOR BUILDING
40 West 40th street between Fifth and Sixth avenues
Raymond Hood, architect. 1924

Raymond Hood's dark and dramatic tribute to heat and furnaces marked an important breakthrough in office design. Rather than build the structure with a blind wall to the west so that a similar building could be constructed against it, Hood reduced the area of the tower and installed windows all the way around the structure, increasing the value of the office space within.

Because Hood disliked the effect of dark windows in a light-colored building, he built the American Radiator Building of black brick, which appears to absorb the windows into its surface, and which serves as a foil for the burst of gold-colored terra cotta flames at the top of the tower.

AMERICAN RADIATOR BUILDING, NEW YORK CITY.

HOT COFFEE

PIES

SECTION OF AUTOMAT MACHINES

Horn & Hardart AUTOMAT — Times Square, New York

HORN & HARDART AUTOMAT
At one time at more than 150 locations in New York
City and Philadelphia
Joseph Horn and Frank Hardart, founders. 1902

Armed with two guiding slogans—"The Public Appreciates Quality" and "Less Work for Mother"—Joseph Horn and Frank Hardart founded their first automated restaurant in Philadelphia in 1902. Ten years later they took their venture to New York City, where it grew into a wildly successful network of self-service restaurants and retail stores.

During Horn & Hardart's prime, the management announced that New Yorkers displayed strong preferences when it came to automated meals: they were passionately devoted to sour cream dressings, chicken pies, strong cheeses, and all seafood except oysters.

Only two Horn & Hardart Automats have managed to survive the competition from McDonald's and Burger King. The larger stands on the southeast corner of 42nd Street and Third Avenue, and there coffee is still dispensed through a nickel-plated dolphin's head.

ONE TIMES SQUARE/ TIMES TOWER

South end of Times Square
Eidlitz & MacKenzie, architects. 1904.
Remodeled by Smith, Smith, Haines,
Lundberg & Waehler. 1966

When the *New York Times* moved into its new building on December 31, 1904, the company marked the occasion with a breathtaking display of fireworks and electric lights. The *Times* awed even itself, reporting the next day that "no more beautiful picture was ever limned in fire on the curtain of midnight." The event established a tradition still observed today. Although the *New York Times* has since moved to West 43rd Street, thousands of revelers continue to celebrate New Year's Eve in Times Square each year.

The building has not been allowed to age gracefully. In 1966 remodelers scraped off its ornate terra cotta exterior and replaced it with stark slabs of white marble virtually unbroken by windows.

Times Building. New York.

614.

THE BOND SIGN

Atop the Bond Clothing Store, on Broadway from
West 44th to West 45th streets.
Douglas Leigh, Inc., designer. 1948. Dismantled 1954

The Bond clothing concern's spellbinding block-long
waterfall sign reigned over Times Square for only six
years, but it burned itself deeply into the memories of
all who saw it. The waterfall, which was illuminated by
more than two miles of neon and 21,500 electric light
bulbs, fell at a rate of fifty thousand gallons a minute,
and required three thousand gallons of antifreeze to
keep it moving in cold weather. The mammoth figures
of a man and woman that flanked the falls weighed more
than six tons each and stood five stories high. By daylight they looked nude; at night they wore electric togas.

Bond's later rented this display area to the Wrigley
Company, which installed its own outrageous sign—an
enormous panel of chewing gum and animated neon
fish. That sign no longer exists, the clothing store has
moved, and in 1980 the building became Bond's Dis-
cothèque.

ROSELAND, "America's Foremost Ballroom-Cafe"
Broadway at 51st Street, New York City

ROSELAND

Original location: northeast corner of West 51st Street
and Broadway. 1919
Present location: 239 West 52nd Street. 1956

Roseland, "New York's Historic Shrine of the Dance,"
has felt the feet of more than 100 million dancers since
it first opened its doors on New Year's Eve, 1919. The
ballroom moved from its original location (pictured
here) to its present building in 1956. Its hallmark is a
truly oceanic maple dance floor that covers nearly half
a city block and can accommodate two thousand dancers
at a time.

A number of dancers, among them Adele Astaire,
Ruby Keeler, and Bill Robinson, have donated their
shoes to Roseland's "Wall of Fame" lobby display,
which is probably the only dancing-shoe museum in
the world. The lobby also contains a list of the names
of over five hundred married couples who first met on
the Roseland dance floor.

30028   Roof Garden. Hotel Astor, New York.

THE HOTEL ASTOR

Broadway between West 44th and West 45th streets
Clinton & Russell, architects. 1904. Replaced by the
Astor Plaza in 1969

The roof garden at William Waldorf Astor's ten-story
Hotel Astor was a spectacular example of the elaborate
open-air cafés that crowned nearly every fine New York
hotel in the first decade of the century. On top of the
Hotel Astor the crème of high society could sip juleps
and lemonade while wandering among vine-covered
pergolas, mock waterfalls, rustic pagodas, exotic floral
displays, and strand after strand of electric lights.

In 1909 the garden at the Astor was doubled in size
and featured full-grown pine and palm trees, an enclosed tearoom for sitting out stormy weather, and a
landing pad for "airships."

It was in a similar roof garden on top of Madison
Square Garden that Harry Thaw shot Stanford White in
1906.

74

The Hippodrome, New York.

THE HIPPODROME

Sixth Avenue between West 43rd and West 44th streets
Frederic Thompson, architect. 1905. Demolished 1939

To the great displeasure of New York's clubmen, the world's largest indoor amusement center reared its head in 1905 in the previously exclusive area known to tourists as "Rubberneck Row"—the home of Delmonico's, Sherry's, the Harvard Club, the Yale Club, and the New York Yacht Club.

Built under the direction of Frederic Thompson—of the theatrical firm of Thompson and Dundy, which built Coney Island's Luna Park—the brick, marble, and steel Hippodrome could seat fifty-three hundred spectators and offered a flood of extravagant entertainments—including diving horses, a re-creation of the Battle of Andersonville (complete with a rushing mountain torrent), somersaulting automobiles, ice shows, aquatic ballets, and a spectacle called "Neptune's Daughter," which featured sixty-four dancing girls who vanished into a tank of water in an elaborate diving bell.

THE WALDORF-ASTORIA HOTEL
301 Park Avenue between East 49th and
East 50th streets
Schultze & Weaver, architects. 1931

In 1931 the Waldorf-Astoria moved uptown
from its 33rd Street site into what was then
the tallest hotel building in the world—
Schultze and Weaver's forty-seven stories of
streamlined Park Avenue elegance.

The new Waldorf featured an underground siding for private railway cars, a ballroom that could be joined with adjacent sa-
lons to form an entertainment suite for up to
six thousand guests, an eighteenth-floor ter-
race with a retractable roof, and what the
management claimed was the largest hand-
tufted rug ever woven in a single piece. The
rug, which represented a Persian garden,
measured seventy by fifty feet, required fifty
men to haul it up the entrance stairs, and
was said to contain 12.6 million knots tied
in a ten-month period by thirty Czechoslo-
vakian workers.

The Waldorf-Astoria Park Avenue Foyer — Murals by Louis Rigal. © Steel Engraved by Joseph Guttman.

On September 27, 1931, Herbert Hoover opened the hotel from his desk in the White House with a nation-wide radio broadcast of welcome and goodwill while detectives guarded the building's entrances from throngs of job seekers. Later in the week six thousand special guests devoured twelve hundred lobsters and a hundred pounds of caviar at the hotel's opening dinner.

In the 1960s much of the building's interior was re-modeled with Edwardian fixtures, but the the Waldorf-Astoria still remains a superb example of the Art Deco style and a very grand hotel.

PHOTO WENDELL MC RAE

ROCKEFELLER CENTER

Bounded by West 48th and West 51st
streets and Fifth and Sixth avenues
Reinhard & Hofmeister; Corbett, Harrison
& Macmurray; Hood, Godley & Fouilhoux;
architects of the original center. 1931–40

Rockefeller Center is remarkable not only
for the beauty of its design, but for the fact
that it was the largest private permanent
construction project conceived and built in
America between the start of the Depression
and the end of World War II. Its original
fourteen buildings are situated on land that
in the early nineteenth century was occupied by the Elgin Botanic Garden; they are
a marvel of unified urban design—a truly
efficient, attractive "skyscraper city." The
center has grown steadily over the past few
decades; it now contains twenty-one office
buildings and a dizzying complex of underground streets, shops, and open public
spaces.

The original plan for the center—later re-
ferred to as the "oilcan" model—called for
a large, cylindrical structure directly east of
the RCA Building. When the bank that was
to occupy the building backed out of the
project, the cylinder was replaced by two
buildings—La Maison Française and the
British Empire Building—separated by
"Channel Gardens," the landscaped prom-
enade that leads from Fifth Avenue to the
sunken Rockefeller Plaza.

Rockefeller Plaza Outdoor Ice Skating Pond, Rockefeller Center New York City

16610

85

The best known of the many sculptures, plaques, and murals that stud the center is Paul Manship's gilt-bronze statue of Prometheus, which soars over the western side of Rockefeller Plaza. The card opposite shows the two smaller male and female figures that originally flanked the statue. They were later moved to the roof garden of the Palazzo d'Italia at 50th Street and Fifth Avenue.

The ice-skating rink in Rockefeller Plaza opened on Christmas Day, 1936. It quickly became one of midtown's most popular attractions and has been immortalized by novelist J. D. Salinger as the scene of Holden Caulfield's memorable date with Sally Hayes in *Catcher in the Rye.* In the summer the rink becomes an open-air café, blooming with patio umbrellas.

RADIO CITY MUSIC HALL

Sixth Avenue at 50th Street
The Rockefeller Center design team with Samuel L.
Rothafel, architects. 1932

The immense Radio City Music Hall was built under the direction of Samuel L. Rothafel, a master showman known to New Yorkers as "Roxy," who defected from his own elaborate Roxy Theater to join the Rockefeller project, which resulted in one of the most sumptuous entertainment palaces of the period.

The theater, which seats sixty-two hundred patrons, features the world's largest theater organ; a stage that can support up to six large elephants; and the Rockettes, a troupe of sixty-four inexhaustible precision dancers who won a grand prize for their sixteen-minute performance at the Paris Exposition of 1937.

The auditorium's special effects are as dazzling as its stage shows. The light orchestrator can project an aurora borealis effect or dozens of other patterns on the painted sunburst ceiling, and the vast curtain can be raised in any of a hundred different configurations.

The management has always found it difficult to book attractions that will keep the cavernous auditorium filled, but the theater consistently attracts capacity crowds to its Thanksgiving, Christmas, and Easter extravaganzas.

62302

12135 INTERIOR OF ST. PATRICK'S CATHEDRAL, NEW YORK. COPR. DETROIT PUBLISHING CO.

ST. PATRICK'S CATHEDRAL

Fifth Avenue between East 50th and East 51st streets
James Renwick, Jr., architect. 1879

When New York was made an archdiocese in 1850, Archbishop John Hughes suggested that a new cathedral be constructed on land that had been purchased by the church in 1828. By the time the cathedral opened its doors in 1879, the site had become prime real estate property, and St. Patrick's found itself in the center of Manhattan's most luxurious residential area.

The cathedral is enormous. The spires, which were completed in 1888, tower 330 feet above Fifth Avenue; the interior measures 307 by 124 feet; the ceiling vault rises 112 feet; and the building seats nearly twenty-five hundred people. Its seventy stained-glass windows were made in France by Henry Ely of Nantes and Nicholas Lorin of Chartres. Forty-five of the windows represent figures; the rest bear cathedral glass in geometric patterns.

In October 1965, Pope Paul VI visited St. Patrick's on the first papal journey to the United States, and Pope John Paul II visited in October 1979.

Uptown

New Plaza Hotel.

THE PLAZA HOTEL

Fifth Avenue between West 58th and West 59th streets
Henry J. Hardenbergh, architect. 1907.
Extension built 1921

Built in 1907 on the site of an earlier, smaller, unassuming Plaza Hotel, Hardenbergh's eighteen-story tribute to Edwardian excellence derives its name from the Grand Army Plaza, which it faces.

During the Plaza's early years, waiters brought hot drinks to guests as they skated in Central Park. That amenity is no longer offered, but the hotel still maintains its reputation as the touchstone of elegant service.

The Plaza's guest register has been luminous from the start. Visitors and residents have included Diamond Jim Brady, Cecil Beaton, Marlene Dietrich, Christian Dior, Somerset Maugham, Zelda and F. Scott Fitzgerald, Frank Lloyd Wright, the Beatles, and that scandalous children's book heroine, Eloise.

Central Park with Majestic Hotel & Dakota Ap. N. Y. City

THE DAKOTA APARTMENTS
One West 72nd Street at Central Park West
Henry J. Hardenbergh, architect. 1884

When Edward Clark began planning a luxury apartment building on New York's Upper West Side, his friends thought he was insane. The idea of lavish apartment dwellings for the rich was a fairly new one, and the site Clark had picked was far from the city's centers of activity. The name "Dakota" was originally suggested to make fun of the isolated location, but Clark adopted it in earnest and had the architect decorate the facade with wheat, corn, and Indian motifs.

From the start the large apartments, well stocked with fireplaces and views of Central Park, attracted an exceptional list of tenants willing to spur the more fashionable East Side. Through the years the roster has included Boris Karloff, Rosemary Clooney, Ruth Ford, Paul Gallico, Judy Garland, Lauren Bacall, Leonard Bernstein, Roberta Flack, John Lennon, and Yoko Ono. The Dakota itself glowed in the spotlight as the bedeviled apartment house in the movie *Rosemary's Baby*.

CENTRAL PARK

Bounded by 59th and 110th streets, Fifth Avenue, and
Central Park West
Frederick Law Olmsted and Calvert Vaux, architects.
1873

The grid plan inflicted on New York by the Street Commission in 1811 left little room for parks and squares; the public was expected to visit the waterfront for fresh air and recreation. However, by the 1840s the waterfront was largely taken up by commercial buildings and docks, and the city was experiencing its first serious problems of overcrowding. In 1844 reformers, led by William Cullen Bryant, called for the creation of a great public park. By 1850 the issue was a political one. Both candidates in that year's mayoral contest promised a park, and the winner, Ambrose Kingsland, was true to his word. By 1857, 840 acres of land had been bought and a design competition announced. Olmsted and Vaux's winning design, "Greensward," offered an enticing man-made complex of valleys, pools, glades, elegant bridges, promenades, and meandering paths—a romantic effect that took nearly twenty years and 10 million horse-cartloads of dirt to achieve.

More than a century after Central Park's creation it still fulfills its promise as a truly grand, public oasis in a congested city. It offers innumerable pleasures, among them concerts, roller skating, sledding, strolling, bicycling, and model-sailboat racing in the pond made famous by E. B. White's heroic storybook mouse, Stuart Little.

A Scene in Central Park, New York.

96-69

E-1229. Museum of Art, Central Park, New York.

THE METROPOLITAN MUSEUM OF ART

Central Park, facing Fifth Avenue between 80th and
84th streets
Central Fifth Avenue facade, Richard Morris Hunt and
Richard Howland Hunt, architects. 1902

In 1870 members of the Union League Club incorpo-
rated the Metropolitan Museum of Art, endowed it with
174 Dutch and French paintings, and found the collection temporary shelter—first in a former dancing acad-
emy on Fifth Avenue, and later in a mansion on 14th
Street. In 1880 the growing collection moved to elegant
permanent quarters designed by Calvert Vaux and Jacob
Wrey Mould, facing Central Park at 82nd Street. That
building has since been altered and obscured by several

additions, most obviously the monumental Fifth Avenue facade designed by Richard M. Hunt and his son, completed in 1902, and by the north and south Fifth Avenue wings designed by McKim, Mead and White and finished in 1926.

The Metropolitan's vast and valuable holdings include encyclopedic collections of European and American paintings and sculpture; an extensive photography and print collection; remarkable installations of Islamic, Greek, and Egyptian art; large decorative arts collections; and the famous yet modest Temple of Dendur. The Roman Court pictured here is now the museum's Fountain Restaurant.

THE AMERICAN MUSEUM OF NATURAL HISTORY

Bounded by West 77th and West 81st streets, Central Park West, and Columbus Avenue
General plan and first wing, Vaux and Mould, architects, 1877; West 77th Street wings, J. C. Cady & Co., architects, 1892–98; and Cady, Berg & See, architects, 1899; additions, 1924, 1926, and 1933

The American Museum of Natural History started life in the Central Park Arsenal, but soon outgrew its quarters there and moved to this location on Manhattan Square.

The museum, which has expanded to become one of the world's greatest showcases of natural history, now displays more than twenty-three hundred exhibits, dioramas, and mounted specimens in its fifty-eight halls. It has also been the scene of a number of extraordinary events—among them a tea party for five hundred held under a dinosaur in 1905 and the theft and subsequent recovery of the Star of India, a 563-carat star sapphire in the museum's spectacular gem collection.

14829

THE CATHEDRAL OF ST. JOHN THE DIVINE

Amsterdam Avenue at West 112th Street
Heins & La Farge, architects, 1892–1911; Cram &
Ferguson, architects, 1911–42. Unfinished

The manufacturer of this postcard was premature in
representing the Cathedral of St. John the Divine so
near completion; only about half of what is pictured
here has actually been built.

Since work began on the cathedral in 1892, plans for
the structure's final appearance have changed many
times. Heins and La Farge directed the construction of
a Byzantine-Romanesque apse and choir; later Ralph
Cram planned for the cathedral to be completed in the
French Gothic style. But by the time of Cram's death in
1941 only the nave and the west facade of the building—
except for the towers—had been completed to his spec-
ifications. World War II called a halt to the construction,
and no work was resumed until 1978.

When it is finished, St. John the Divine will be the
largest cathedral in the world.

GENERAL U. S. GRANT MONUMENT AND TOMB, NEW YORK

1926. ILL. POST CARD CO., N. Y.

GRANT'S TOMB
Riverside Drive at West 122nd Street
John H. Duncan, architect. 1897

After Ulysses S. Grant died in 1885, the military made a plea to bury his body in Arlington National Cemetery, but was overruled by Mrs. Grant, who explained that her husband himself had chosen New York as his final resting place, because the city had been kind to him in his time of troubles, and because Mrs. Grant could later be buried there by his side.

Grant was interred in a temporary vault while funds were raised from ninety thousand subscribers to build the structure, and his sarcophagus was finally moved to the tomb in April 1897. The sarcophagus containing the remains of Mrs. Grant was placed next to it in 1902.

Near the tomb's West Driveway, a small stone urn "Erected to the Memory of an Amiable Child," memorializes a five-year-old who fell to his death from the rocks here in 1797. When the child's family sold the property, it asked that the grave never be disturbed, a request that has been honored ever since.

THE POLO GROUNDS

Harlem River Drive at East 155th Street
Constructed 1911. Demolished 1964

The old New York Giants baseball team first played on a former polo field at 110th Street and Fifth Avenue, and, when they moved to their Coogan's Bluff location in the 1890s, they named their new lot the Polo Grounds for sentimental reasons. A fire in 1911 forced the Giants to rebuild their park, and when the stadium was finished it was the biggest one of its time, with a seating capacity of fifty-four thousand.

In 1913 the New York Yankees became the tenants of the Giants, and it was at the Polo Grounds over the next several years that they grew from a third-rate team to the force they are today. In 1920 Babe Ruth joined the Yankees, and the next year the Yankees and Giants faced each other in the World Series—both playing on home territory, the Polo Grounds. In 1923 the Yankees moved to their present stadium. The Giants abandoned their old home in 1957 to become a San Francisco team.

4437-29

THE GEORGE WASHINGTON BRIDGE

The Hudson River, from West 179th Street in
Manhattan to Fort Lee, New Jersey
Othmar H. Ammann, engineer; Cass Gilbert, architect.
1931

When the George Washington Bridge was built, its
thirty-five-hundred-foot span was twice the length of
any existing bridge. Each of its four main cables measures a yard in diameter, a mile in length, and with its
protective covering weighs 14 million pounds. Governor Franklin D. Roosevelt called it "our most impressive and characteristic landmark," and Le Corbusier
lauded it as "the most beautiful bridge in the world."

If it had been built as planned, the bridge's towers
would be faced in granite, as in the card above. But as

5A-H647

the final stages of construction began, the Port Authority responded to public sentiment—and to the obvious cost savings—by leaving the steel towers bare.

The Port Authority allowed the public the final word on the bridge's name as well by announcing in early 1931 that it would heed the results of a write-in election. Forty-five letters came in for the "Palisades Bridge," and others suggested the "Mother's Bridge" and the "Prosperity Bridge," but the name "George Washington Bridge" won with twenty-seven letters, one of which contained the signatures of 1,062 schoolchildren. When the bridge opened to the public on October 24, 1931, two boys on roller skates were the first to cross. The Will Rogers Memorial Beacon for Aviators is shown on the card above.

THE CLOISTERS
Fort Tryon Park, Broadway north of 193rd Street
Charles Collens of Allen, Collens & Willis, assembler
of the medieval structures. 1938

In 1925 John D. Rockefeller, Jr., donated funds to the
Metropolitan Museum of Art for the purchase of the
George Grey Barnard collection of medieval architectural artifacts, to which he added forty medieval sculptures from his own collection. Later he gave the city
Fort Tryon Park and the wherewithal to build the Cloisters, the gemlike museum of medieval art perched on
the park's northern hilltop. To protect the museum's
magnificent view of the Palisades, Rockefeller acquired
seven hundred acres of land just across the Hudson and
presented them to the Palisades Interstate Park Commission.

The museum, which is composed of a quartet of European cloisters linked by several chapels, halls, and
rooms, contains an exemplary collection of medieval
treasures, including the Unicorn Tapestries and Roger
Campin's exquisite Annunciation altarpiece.

Environs

1958   THE CONSERVATORIES, BRONX PARK, NEW YORK

NEW YORK BOTANICAL GARDEN

Bronx Park, North of East Fordham Road
Calvert Vaux and Samuel Parsons, Jr., architects, 1895;
William R. Cobb for Lord & Burnham, architect of the
Conservatory, 1902

Spread over 240 acres at the north end of Bronx Park,
the Botanical Garden harbors a beautiful section of the
Bronx River Gorge, a virgin hemlock forest, and more
than twelve thousand species of plants. The Conservatory, which echoes the noble and delicate lines of the
Great Palm House at Kew and Paxton's Crystal Palace
in London, features a central Palm House that arches to
a stunning height of ninety feet, offering visitors one of
New York's most exhilarating visual experiences.

In 1978 the Conservatory was renamed after Enid A.
Haupt, who funded its restoration.

229:–LINE UP OF PLANES, LA GUARDIA FIELD, NEW YORK MUNICIPAL AIRPORT

ADMINISTRATION BUILDING, NEW YORK MUNICIPAL AIRPORT, NORTH BEACH, NEW YORK CITY   46978

LAGUARDIA AIRPORT

North Beach, Queens
Original buildings and Marine Terminal, Delano and Aldrich, architects. 1939; New Central Terminal and Central Tower, Harrison & Abramovitz, architects. 1965

Mayor Fiorello LaGuardia (the "Little Flower"), was elected to office in 1933 with a campaign promise to build his city an airport. Rankled by the fact that the Newark airport served the city of New York, he took on the matter as a personal crusade; on one occasion he refused to leave a plane at Newark because the destination on his ticket read New York.

LaGuardia's work paid off in December, 1939, when the North Beach Airport opened with service by American, United, and Trans World Airlines. The airport, the largest and most efficient in the world, was quickly renamed "LaGuardia" as a tribute to its energetic supporter.

CONEY ISLAND
Southern Brooklyn

At the peak of its popularity—from the time Steeplechase Park opened in 1897 until Dreamland was destroyed by fire in 1911—Coney Island attracted more pleasure seekers and notoriety than any other amusement area in the United States. On a typical summer weekend an average of five hundred thousand to seven hundred thousand visitors made the trip to the island, and on particularly torrid nights thousands fled the heat of the city to sleep on Coney's beaches.

For the first decade of this century three amusement parks dominated Coney Island—Steeplechase Park, Luna Park, and Dreamland—and each successive park offered diversions more thrilling and spectacular than the last. Reenactments of catastrophes and pageants proved irresistibly popular; visitors could witness the Fall of Pompeii, the Galveston Flood of 1900, the Johnstown Flood of 1889, and the Destruction of San Francisco. Or they could watch a full-scale re-creation of the Durbar Celebration in the Streets of Delhi, which boasted sixty elephants (including the largest one in captivity), forty camels, three hundred native Hindus, one hundred horsemen, and five hundred foot soldiers.

The parks bristled with an eye-popping, stomach-wrenching variety of mechanical amusement rides, including a simulated elevator crash; the Switchback Railroad (which later evolved into the roller coaster); Shoot-the-Chutes; Loop-the-Loop; Witching Waves (an ordeal devised by the inventor of the revolving door); and the Steeplechase, an extended hobbyhorse ride.

Crowd of Bathers on Beach, front of Steeplechase, Coney Island, N. Y.

DREAMLAND. CONEY ISLAND.

In 1906 a man named Sam Friede announced the imminent construction of what would be Coney Island's most breathtaking sight of all—the seven-hundred-foot Globe Tower, a spherical architectural marvel that would contain a vaudeville theater, an aerial hippodrome, a five-ring circus, a revolving restaurant, a hotel, an observatory, and a telegraph station. Funds were never raised to build the structure, and it later appeared that the entire promotion had been a hoax.

In 1907 fire swept Steeplechase Park and destroyed thirty-five acres of Coney Island. In 1911 an even more disastrous blaze broke out in one of Dreamland's rides and swiftly burned the entire park to the ground. Coney Island never really recovered from the loss, which was compounded four years later by the death of Luna Park's owner and his partner's subsequent bankruptcy. Steeplechase Park declined in the 1920s, and by the 1940s the island had deteriorated into the handful of not-as-spectacular carnival entertainments and hot-dog concessions found there today.

2621   THE STEEL GLOBE TOWER, 700 FEET HIGH, CONEY ISLAND, N. Y.

WFS

THE TRYLON AND THE PERISPHERE,
KEY BUILDINGS OF THE NEW YORK WORLD'S FAIR OF
AT NIGHT

(C) N Y W F

THE 1939 NEW YORK WORLD'S FAIR

1,216 acres in Flushing Meadow, Queens

It took dozens of committees nearly three years to design the 1939 New York World's Fair, an elaborate and outrageously expensive exposition dedicated to "Building the World of Tomorrow." The Fair's symbol, the austere white Theme Center, was composed of the Trylon (a 610-foot tower) and the Perisphere (a globe 180 feet in diameter), structures which Fair officials claimed represented the "all-inclusive World of Tomorrow" and a "Pointer to Infinity." The Trylon and Perisphere were encircled by the Helicline, a 950-foot walkway. At night the Theme Center served as a mammoth screen on which colored lights—amber, then red, then blue—were projected; and lighting experts provided special illuminations for special occasions, among them a portrait of Thomas Edison to mark his birthday, and a red, white, and blue pattern for the Fourth of July.

Other structures at the Fair were just as extraordinary. The Cosmetics Building looked like a giant powder puff, the Marine Transportation Building featured two enormous ocean-liner prows, the Carrier Corporation housed its air-conditioning exhibit in an outsize igloo, and the National Cash Register Company's circular structure was topped by the "world's largest cash register," which kept a tally of the Fair's daily visitors.

THE 1964 NEW YORK WORLD'S FAIR
646 acres in Flushing Meadow, Queens

At twilight on April 22, 1964, a 12 billion-candlepower beam of light penetrated the heavens over Flushing Meadow, the world's largest fountain burst into colored light below a shower of fireworks, and a 610-bell carillon rang out "There's No Business Like Show Business," opening another New York World's Fair. On the site of the old Trylon and Perisphere stood the new fair's symbol, the Unisphere—described by some as the world's largest bird cage—and circling the grounds was a four-thousand-foot-long monorail, a futuristic hanging railroad. The General Motors "Futurama" ride, entered through a canopy resembling a giant tailfin, was the most popular at the fair, drawing some 15 million visitors in the first season alone. Unlike the earlier Trylon and Perisphere, the Unisphere has survived as a permanent landmark in Queens.

Publishers and Dates of the Postcards

On Collecting New York City Postcards

Old New York City postcards can be found with varying degrees of success at flea markets and antique stores and through organizations of postcard collectors. Prices range from five cents to more than twenty dollars, depending on the age and rarity of the card and the conscience and savvy of the seller. Flea markets and the less polished antique stores are the most likely sources of bargains, once you know how to spot them.

Postcard collectors' clubs exist in many cities, and their meetings are the best places to find old postcards in quantity, including New York City cards, and to get a sense of the range of prices and values. Almost all of the postcards in this book were found at the meetings of the Metropolitan Post Card Collectors' Club of New York City or lent by members of the club, which meets on the first Friday of each month at the Prince George Hotel, 14 East 28th Street, in Manhattan. If you are in New York on the first Friday of the month, a trip to the Prince George is a recommended treat, if only as a chance to witness the tremendous variety of postcard styles available for collecting. The doors open at 5:00 P.M. To find out if a postcard club exists in your area, send a stamped, self-addressed envelope with your inquiry to: Post Card Club Federation, John H. Mc-Clinton, Director, Box 27, Somerdale, New Jersey 08083.

For the visitor to New York City—and for the resident—the store called Welcome to New York in Greenwich Village is certainly worth investigation. The management always keeps several categorized boxes filled with old New York City postcards.

Generally speaking, the older New York City postcards are more valuable than the newer ones, many of which are still made and can be found on postcard racks in card shops and newsstands throughout the city. Common cards of major sights dating from the 1910-era postcard boom through the linen era of the 1940s range in price from ten cents to a dollar. Higher prices are charged for pre-1902 postcards, cards by collectible publishers like Detroit and Rotograph, and cards of hard-to-find sights, buildings never built, or images made from plans that changed before construction. Unusual mechanical postcards with moving pieces, hold-to-light cards with tiny built-in windows, and other specially made cards command the highest prices of all.

One further twist to postcard collecting is that the presence of such objects as early trucks, airplanes, or zeppelins on cards can increase their value dramatically, sometimes to the dismay of the New York City postcard collector who may only be interested in the building in front of which the rare truck is parked.

If you are interested in reading more about postcard collecting or the history of postcards, the most complete book on the subject is *Picture Postcards in the United States 1893–1918* by George and Dorothy Miller (New York: Clarkson N. Potter, 1976). Another useful and thorough guide for the beginner is *The Book of Postcard Collecting* by Thomas E. Range (New York: E. P. Dutton, 1980) which has the added advantage of being peppered with illustrations of New York City postcards, since the author is an avid New York collector himself. The Gotham Book Mart stocks all available books and journals about postcards, and sells them through the mail. Visit in person or write for a catalogue at 41 West 47th Street, New York, NY 10036.

Index to the Sights

Acknowledgments

The following people very kindly lent postcards from their private collections. The author wishes to extend them thanks for their generosity and help, without which the book could never have been published:

Marilyn Jensen (whose postcard appears on p. 89)

Gary Wright (whose postcard appears on p. 60)

Thomas E. Range (whose postcards appear on pp. 17, 22, 23, 24, 28, 38, 39, 41, 42, 44, 47, 49, 52, 55, 57, 65, 66, 67, 72, 73, 74, 76, 77, 79, 85, 93, 94, 96)

For help in researching the cards and the text, thanks are extended to Kathryn Greenthal of The Metropolitan Museum of Art, Helen A. Harrison of The Queens Museum, Eli Katz of Bond Clothes, Michael Langenstein, the members of the Metropolitan Postcard Collectors' Club, the staffs of the New York Public Library and the Boston Public Library, John Neyenesch, Caroline Weintz, and Walter Weintz.

Thanks to Eleanor Caponigro and Susan Marsh for their helpful suggestions about the book's design.

Special thanks to Polly Cone, Eric Kampmann, and Lori Marsh.